POCKET BOOK OF

# HAPPINESS

WELBECK
BALANCE

A Trigger Book
Published by Welbeck Balance
An imprint of Welbeck Publishing Group
20 Mortimer Street
London W1T 3JW

First published by Trigger Publishing in 2020
Reprinted by Welbeck Balance in 2021

A CIP catalogue record for this book is available from the British Library

ISBN
Hardback – 978-1-80129-107-1

Cover design and typeset by Fusion Graphic Design Ltd

Printed by RRD in Dongguan, China

10 9 8 7 6 5 4 3 2 1

**Note/Disclaimer**

**www.welbeckpublishing.com**

POCKET BOOK OF

# HAPPINESS

WELBECK
BALANCE

# INTRODUCTION

Modern life can be filled with so much: from the daily commute, a hectic schedule and cooking an evening meal; to those crucial turning points: quitting your job, moving house, finding love. Between the noise, it can be hard to stop and recognise those all-important moments of joy.

The *Pocket Book of Happiness* offers a little guidance for when the scales of life are tipped, times become turbulent and a moment of reflection is needed. From the minds of some of the world's most well-known figures, learn to find your footing, take a breath and feel happy once more.

Don't ever underestimate the importance you
can have because history has shown
us that courage can be contagious and hope
can take on a life of its own

**Michelle Obama**

He who lives in harmony with himself
lives in harmony with the universe

Marcus Aurelius

But I know, somehow, that only when
it is dark enough can you see the stars

**Martin Luther King Jr.**

Doing what you like is freedom.
Liking what you do is happiness

**Frank Tyger**

I, not events, have the power to make me happy or unhappy today. I can choose which it shall be. Yesterday is dead, tomorrow hasn't arrived yet ...

... I have just one day, today,
and I'm going to be happy in it

**Groucho Marx**

You might not make it to the top, but if you are doing what you love, there is much more happiness there than being rich or famous

**Tony Hawks**

It's part of life to have obstacles.
It's about overcoming obstacles;
that's the key to happiness

Herbie Hancock

Our greatest happiness does not depend on the condition of life in which chance has placed us, but is always the result of a good conscience, good health ...

... occupation, and freedom
in all just pursuits

**Thomas Jefferson**

The pursuit of happiness is a most
ridiculous phrase: if you pursue happiness
you'll never find it

**Carrie Snow**

Happiness is secured through virtue;
it is a good attained by man's own will

Thomas Aquinas

Understanding your employee's perspective can go a long way towards increasing productivity and happiness

**Kathryn Minshew**

The greater part of our happiness
or misery depends on our dispositions
and not on our circumstances.
We carry the seeds of the one
or the other about with us in our
minds wherever we go

**Martha Washington**

Life is not a problem to be
solved but a reality to be experienced

**Søren Kierkegaard**

The moments of happiness we enjoy
take us by surprise. It is not that we seize
them, but that they seize us

**Ashley Montagu**

Nothing brings me more happiness
than trying to help the most vulnerable
people in society

**Princess Diana**

We all want to help one another. Human beings are like that. We want to live by each other's happiness, not by each other's misery

**Charlie Chaplin**

Action may not bring happiness but
there is no happiness without action

**William James**

There is no such thing as the pursuit of happiness, but there is the discovery of joy

Joyce Grenfell

For every minute you are angry you
lose sixty seconds of happiness

**Ralph Waldo Emerson**

Happiness, not in another place
but this place ... not for another hour,
but this hour

**Walt Whitman**

Actions are right in proportion as they tend to promote happiness; wrong as they tend to produce the reverse of happiness ...

... By happiness is intended pleasure
and the absence of pain

**John Stuart Mill**

It's not possible to experience constant
euphoria, but if you're grateful,
you can find happiness in everything

**Pharrell Williams**

Folks are usually about as happy as they make their minds up to be

Abraham Lincoln

Don't forget to tell yourself positive things daily! You must love yourself internally to glow externally

**Hannah Bronfman**

It's in responsibility that most people find the meaning that sustains them through life. It's not in happiness. It's not in impulsive pleasure

**Jordan Peterson**

In our lives, change is unavoidable,
loss is unavoidable. In the adaptability and
ease with which we experience change,
lies our happiness and freedom

**Buddha**

I don't have to take a trip around the world
or be on a yacht in the Mediterranean to have
happiness. I can find it in the little things,
like looking out into my backyard and
seeing deer in the fields

**Queen Latifah**

When you relinquish the desire to control
your future, you can have more happiness

**Nicole Kidman**

Happiness is not doing fun things.
Happiness is doing meaningful things

**Maxime Lagacé**

If you aren't grateful for what you
already have, what makes you think you
would be happy with more

**Roy T. Bennett**

No matter what you're going through,
there's a light at the end of the tunnel and it
may seem hard to get to it but you can

Demi Lovato

My mother is a big believer in being responsible for your own happiness. She always talked about finding joy in small moments ...

... and insisted that we stop and tak
in the beauty of an ordinary day

**Jennifer Garner**

Now and then it's good to pause in our
pursuit of happiness and just be happy

Guillaume Apollinaire

It's the moments that I stopped just
to be, rather than do, that have
given me true happiness

**Richard Branson**

Stay positive and happy.
Work hard and don't give up hope.
Be open to criticism and keep learning ...

... Surround yourself with happy,
warm and genuine people

**Tena Desae**

I must learn to be content with
being happier than I deserve

**Jane Austen**

You cannot prevent the
birds of sadness from passing
over your head ...

... but you can prevent their making a nest in your hair

**Chinese proverb**

Three grand essentials to happiness in this
life are something to do, something to love,
and something to hope for

**Joseph Addison**

Success is getting what you want.
Happiness is wanting what you get

Dale Carnegie

The most important thing is to
enjoy your life – to be happy
– it's all that matters

**Audrey Hepburn**

If you want to be happy,
set a goal that commands your thoughts,
liberates your energy and inspires your hopes

**Andrew Carnegie**

Do not anticipate trouble,
or worry about what may never happen

**Benjamin Franklin**

Doing what you were born to do ...
that's the way to be happy

**Agnes Martin**

It is not how much we have, but how much we enjoy, that makes happiness

**Charles Spurgeon**

I am content; that is a blessing
greater than riches;
and he to whom that is given
need ask no more

**Henry Fielding**

The more grateful I am,
the more beauty I see

**Mary Davis**

Wine is constant proof that
God loves us and loves to see us happy

Benjamin Franklin

Happiness quite unshared can scarcely
be called happiness; it has no taste

**Charlotte Brontë**

All happiness depends on courage and work

**Honoré de Balzac**

The foolish man seeks happiness in the distance, the wise grows it under his feet

James Oppenheim

Being happy never goes out of fashion

**Lilly Pulitzer**

The mere sense of living is joy enough

**Emily Dickinson**

Happiness is a place between
too much and too little

**Finnish proverb**

Simplicity makes me happy

**Alicia Keys**

Happiness depends upon ourselves

**Aristotle**

The secret of health for
both mind and body is not
to mourn for the past,
worry about the future,
or anticipate troubles ...

... but to live in the present
moment wisely and earnestly

**Buddha**

There is only one happiness in this life,
to love and be loved

George Sand
(a.k.a. Amantine Lucile Aurore Dupin)

You're a happy fellow,
for you'll give happiness and joy to
many other people. There is nothing
better or greater than that!

**Ludwig van Beethoven**

Be happy for this moment.
This moment is your life

**Omar Khayyam**

I think everybody should get
rich and famous and do everything
they ever dreamed of ...

... so they can see that it's not the answer

**Jim Carrey**

Happiness is a gift and the trick is not to
expect it, but to delight in it when it comes

**Charles Dickens**

It is the very mark of the spirit of rebellion
to crave for happiness in this life

**Henrik Ibsen**

Happiness consists more in
conveniences of pleasure that
occur every day than in
great pieces of good fortune that
happen but seldom

**Benjamin Franklin**

Be happy with what you have and are,
be generous with both, and you
won't have to hunt for happiness

**William E. Gladstone**

There is no cosmetic for
beauty like happiness

**Lady Blessington**

It is difficult to find happiness
within oneself, but it is impossible
to find it anywhere else

**Arthur Schopenhauer**

Sometimes we don't find the thing
that will make us happy because we can't
give up the thing that was supposed to

**Robert Brault**

All life is an experiment.
The more experiments you
make the better

Ralph Waldo Emerson

The greatest happiness of life is
the conviction that we are loved;
loved for ourselves, or rather,
loved in spite of ourselves

**Victor Hugo**

Spread love everywhere you go.
Let no one ever come without
leaving happier

**Mother Teresa**

You are responsible for your life.
You can't keep blaming somebody
else for your dysfunction.
Life is really about moving on

**Oprah Winfrey**

The happiness of life is made up of the
little charities of a kiss or smile, a kind look,
a heartfelt compliment

Samuel Taylor Coleridge

The habit of being happy enables
one to be freed, or largely freed, from the
domination of outward conditions

**Robert Louis Stevenson**

All happiness or unhappiness
solely depends upon the
quality of the object to which
we are attached by love

**Baruch Spinoza**

There is no happiness like that of
being loved by your fellow creatures,
and feeling that your presence
is an addition to their comfort

**Charlotte Brontë**

The most wasted of all days
is one without laughter

**Nicolas Chamfort**

Happiness is the best makeup

Drew Barrymore

Happiness is having a large,
loving, caring, close-knit family
in another city

**George Burns**

Even a happy life cannot be without a measure of darkness, and the word happy would lose its meaning if it were not balanced by sadness ...

... It is far better to take things as they come along with patience and equanimity

**Carl Jung**

The pain of parting is nothing
to the joy of meeting again

**Charles Dickens**

With freedom, books, flowers,
and the moon, who could not be happy

**Oscar Wilde**

Roll with the punches and enjoy
every minute of it

**Meghan Markle, Duchess of Sussex**

Man is fond of counting his troubles,
but he does not count his joys.
If he counted them up as he ought to
he would see that every lot
has enough happiness provided for it

**Fyodor Dostoevsky**

Don't waste a minute not being HAPPY.
If one window closes, run to the next
window or break down a door

**Brooke Shields**

The happiness of your life depends upon the quality of your thoughts

**Marcus Aurelius**

With mirth and laughter let
old wrinkles come

William Shakespeare

I relate to happiness as an
ecstatic moment – something you
don't create, you encounter

**Yoko Ono**

If you want to be happy, be

**Leo Tolstoy**

Independence is happiness

**Susan B. Anthony**

Forget not that the earth delights to
feel your bare feet and the winds long
to play with your hair

**Kahil Gibran**

I think the saddest people always
try their hardest to make people happy
because they know what it's like to
feel absolutely worthless ...

... and they don't want anyone
else to feel like that

**Robin Williams**

Most of us are just about as happy
as we make up our minds to be

**William Adams**

To be content means that you
realize you contain what you seek

**Alan Cohen**

Happiness is when what you think, what you say and what you do are in harmony

**Mahatma Gandhi**

If you can laugh, you can get through it

**Jami Gertz**

My family didn't have a lot of money,
and I'm grateful for that.
Money is the longest route to happiness

Evangeline Lilly

Real happiness is not of temporary enjoyment, but is so interwoven with the future that it blesses for ever

**James Lendall Basford**

True happiness is not attained
through self-gratification, but through
fidelity to a worthy purpose

**Helen Keller**

Blessed are those who can
give without remembering and take
without forgetting

**Bernard Meltzer**

We act as though comfort and luxury
were the chief requirements in life,
when all we need to make us really happy
is something to be enthusiastic about

**Charles Kingsley**

Success at the highest level comes
down to one question: Can you decide
that your happiness can come from
someone else's success

**Bill Walton**

Happiness lies in the joy of achievement
and the thrill of creative effort

**Franklin D. Roosevelt**

The true secret of happiness lies in taking a genuine interest in all the details of daily life

William Morris

The worst part of success is trying to find someone who is happy for you

**Bette Midler**

Happiness can only be achieved
by looking inward & learning to enjoy
whatever life has and this requires
transforming greed into gratitude

**Henry Fielding**

Happiness is where we find it,
but very rarely where we seek it

**J. Petit Senn**

Time you enjoy wasting
is not wasted time

Marthe Troly-Curtin

Optimism is a happiness magnet.
If you stay positive, good things and good
people will be drawn to you

**Mary Lou Retton**

The only thing that will make you
happy is being happy with who you are

Goldie Hawn

Be content with what you have;
rejoice in the way things are.
When you realize there is nothing lacking,
the whole world belongs to you

**Lao Tzu**

Happiness depends more on the
inward disposition of mind than on
outward circumstances

**Benjamin Franklin**

My happiness grows in direct proportion
to my acceptance, and in inverse
proportion to my expectations

**Michael J. Fox**

The talent for being happy is appreciating
and liking what you have,
instead of what you don't have

**Woody Allen**

Remember that the happiest
people are not those getting more,
but those giving more

H. Jackson Brown, Jr

For a little guidance elsewhere ...

POCKET BOOK OF

FRIENDSHIP

For when life gets a little tough

# POCKET BOOK OF

# HOPE

For when life gets a little tough

# ABOUT US

Welbeck Balance publishes books dedicated to changing lives. Our mission is to deliver life-enhancing books to help improve your wellbeing so that you can live your life with greater clarity and meaning, wherever you are on life's journey. Our Trigger books are specifically devoted to opening up conversations about mental health and wellbeing.

Welbeck Balance and Trigger are part of the Welbeck Publishing Group – a globally recognized independent publisher based in London. Welbeck are renowned for our innovative ideas, production values and developing long-lasting content. Our books have been translated into over 30 languages in more than 60 countries around the world.

If you love books, then join the club and sign up to our newsletter for exclusive offers, extracts, author interviews and more information.

www.welbeckpublishing.com          www.triggerhub.org

🐦 welbeckpublish                    🐦 Triggercalm
📷 welbeckpublish                    📷 Triggercalm
f welbeckuk                          f Triggercalm

WELBECK
BALANCE